Choose to Change: Start With You

14 Tweaks for Self-Esteem and Confidence

Jacqui Penn

Copyright © 2021 Jacqui Penn

The author or authors assert their moral right under the Copyright, Designs and Patents Act, 1988, to be identified as the author or authors of this work.

All rights reserved. No part of this publication may be reproduced, copied, stored in a retrieval system, or transmitted, in any form or by any means, without the prior written consent of the copyright holder, nor be otherwise circulated in any form of binding or cover other than that in which it is published and without a similar condition being imposed on the subsequent purchaser.

This book is not a substitute for professional medical advice.

Contents

Choose to Change: 1

Copyright © 2021 Jacqui Penn 2

Introduction 5

Chapter 1 - Your inner voice 9

Chapter 2 – Limitations 15

Chapter 3 - Courage 19

Chapter 4 – Regrets 24

Chapter 5 – Confidence 30

Chapter 6 - Do you want anything enough? 36

How are you doing? 40

Part 2 - 43

Chapter 7 - Happiness is inside you 43

Chapter 8 - Are you fulfilled? 48

Chapter 9 - What are you going to do? 53

Chapter 10 - Are you in the system? 57

Chapter 11 – Meditation 61

Chapter 12 - Obstacles or Opportunities 66

Chapter 13 – Shame 70

Chapter 14 - Questions to ask yourself 73

Chapter 15 – Conclusion 76

Your Checklist 79

Exercise List 80

Links 84

Acknowledgements 85
About Jacqui 87
Other Books by Jacqui Penn 87

Introduction

I had a light-up moment when I wrote an author bio for my first book in the Choose to Change series. I wrote the book intending to pass on good vibes and I've had many people telling me it made a difference to them. Brilliant! That was what I'd hoped for.

I wrote in the bio that I always bounce back, and it's true, but then I started to wonder, why? Why doesn't everyone bounce back? We all have to deal with what life throws our way, so what makes some people able to keep going while others struggle?

Why do some people have the ability to move forward and let things go? I'm not indifferent, I always voice my opinions, so it's not that I don't care. I do. I get angry, sad, and wound up, just like everyone else, but the difference is the way I deal with those thoughts. I'm comfortable with having emotions, but not hanging on to them and beating myself up over them.

Every time you hang on to something that's happened, your inner voice shouts, *hey, you should have said this, you could have done that, why didn't you stand up for yourself, you're weak, pathetic, why aren't you stronger?* Am I right? We've all got that nagging inner voice going at it 24/7. This is the part that stops you from loving yourself. It plants doubt that you're good enough, strong enough, nice enough and this is what needs to change.

If one of your friends kept putting you down, you'd want to be as far away from them as possible. Yet, every day you let this inner voice put you down, and you listen. Yes, you do! You even believe what it tells you. Your inner voice needs to stop taunting you, and you can choose to stop the negative vibes it repeatedly sends to you.

I'm happy with myself, and in the long term, no person or event can change that. It took a long time for me to get to where I am today, and it's only in hindsight that I realised my inner voice has always been there, chipping away, until I stopped it.

I found inner happiness and love, which means I don't need other people to make my happiness. I love who I am. That doesn't mean other people don't love me, they do, and it's all relevant.

I'm sharing my thoughts and ideas on loving yourself first because I sincerely believe you have to love yourself before you can love others. You have to start with you.

This book is not for those who aren't wanting or willing to change. It's not for people who are happy where they are already.

This book is for you if you want to change your inner voice, and stop believing everything it tells you. It's for you if you want to believe in yourself.

Start today and challenge yourself to a happier, content outlook on life.

Do the exercises! If you're serious about wanting to make changes, please, don't skip them. I've put a list at the end to make it easy.

There is a handy checklist PDF offer, for you to download, at the end of the book. It will help you to keep track of where you are on your journey, what you want to revisit, and what you've accomplished.

"Discovering who you are today is the first step to being who you will be tomorrow."

-Destiny's Odyssey

Chapter 1 - Your inner voice

"Turn down the volume of your negative inner voice and create a nurturing inner voice to take its place."

–Beverly Engel

It's like you have a constant companion. Someone nattering on in the background, and only you can hear what they say. It could be suggested that because no one else can hear the voice, it's something to be thankful for. You wouldn't want anyone to hear the way it reprimands, nags, criticises, torments and disturbs you. Why do you keep hearing repeats of conversations you wish you'd never had, or wish you'd handled differently?

There are things you wish you could change, and in hindsight, we could all live in a perfect world. That's the problem. No one is perfect; and who would want to be that boring?

Do you want to keep mulling over everything; why doesn't that voice stop nagging and leave you alone? It rarely seems to remind you of pleasant conversations or situations, it usually dwells on the ones you want to forget.

Why did you say *that*, when you could have easily said *this*? Why did you do *that*? You're never going to live *that* down. You made yourself look like a fool. Why can't you be kinder, caring, sympathetic, considerate, thoughtful, and the list goes on. The voice nags at you to be better, tells you you're not good enough, but you know what? You are who you are, and no apologies are necessary.

If you take notice of that voice each time it intrudes, then you are your own worst enemy. You wouldn't take that sort of abuse from a friend, colleague or family member, would you? Maybe you would, and that's another problem for another book.

The thing is, if you can't be true to yourself, who can you be true to? When, whatever it was came blurting out of your mouth, when you decided to do whatever you did, it was your decision at the time, and there was a reason for it. Sometimes, things don't turn out the way we mean and then it's time for honesty and time to put it right. However, we usually react to something, and then later our bravado lets us down, and we want to backtrack because we want others to like who we are.

You don't need to berate yourself or let that inner voice keep reprimanding you. You need to make a decision. Ask yourself one question. Why? Why did you say, do, or think something you've since regretted because that inner voice won't let you move on?

Why does it matter that you spoke the truth, or acted the way you thought best at the time? It's because your inner voice is causing you to doubt yourself.

Don't get me wrong, there have been times, and plenty of them, like when I complained about a child screaming its head off, saying to a fellow helper at a gym club, 'how awful, whose child is that?' The fellow helper and mum of said child burst into tears. I wished the ground had opened up and swallowed me.

I apologised for upsetting her, but it was too late. Later, I didn't regret what I said, as the constant screaming was awful and spoiling the atmosphere, and after that day, the child always behaved impeccably. I did feel bad for upsetting the mum and we became good friends. She confided later that, the child had ruled her until that day, then she got a grip, made a few changes and hey-presto, a lovely little girl emerged. The point is that I didn't let my inner voice control me. I took control and it worked out. That doesn't mean I´m the kind of person that will deliberately upset anyone, but I could have made any number of excuses for saying what I did and felt guilty about it forevermore.

The lesson here is to be true to yourself. Don't change for anyone. You are who you are and you should embrace the fact that you are unique. There isn't another you and no one is in your head except you. So don't feel guilty and let what other people think influence your thoughts. In reality, people should like you for who you are, not what they, or you, think you should be.

The sort of people you want in your life are those that accept you, warts and all.

So when that inner voice pops up uninvited and starts kicking off, you kick right back. You know why! Why you had that thought, opened your mouth or jumped in with two big feet. Don't make excuses. Stand up for yourself and believe in yourself. Don't let that inner voice criticize and put you down. You don't have to be afraid, you are who you are, and you need to embrace what makes you who you are.

That same inner voice can spout off and make personal, hurtful remarks. Your body is too fat, too thin. You're not pretty or handsome, your nose, eyes, chin, hair, skin, legs, and on and on. How do you think someone would feel if you told them what you felt was wrong with their body image? Pretty bad, and you'd have most likely lost a friend. So why hurt yourself, when you wouldn't do it to anyone else. You are the best friend you have and you need to be kind to yourself.

Everyone has an inner voice, and it's a good thing, but stop listening to that inner voice when it makes you feel bad, and stop believing it. Why should you pay attention to a voice determined to make you miserable? Put an end to the negativity. Answer back, put that condemning, interfering opinion in its rightful place. Let your inner voice make you feel good.

Start right here and now and love yourself. That's right, it might feel strange to say the words, but start to love yourself and the rest will follow. Like, and love who you are, and be grateful there is only one you who truly understands how you feel.

Exercise: Challenge your inner voice every time it puts you down, and stop believing what it tells you. Make this small step towards loving and accepting who you are.

Chapter 2 – Limitations

"I define a 'good person' as somebody who is fully conscious of their own limitations. They know their strengths, but they also know their 'shadow' - they know their weaknesses. In other words, they understand that there is no good without bad."

-John Bradshaw

Do you have a plan for your life? Some people are happy to jog along, while others are ambitious and always seem to be chasing a dream. Whether you make conscious life choices or not, doesn't matter. What does matter is that you are doing what is right for you.

Do you feel envious of people who appear to be dynamic in all they do? Do you find yourself wondering why you can't succeed in all you do? Firstly, what you see is not always reality. Some people are good at making you see what they want you to see.

Secondly, all the time you feel envious, or even wish you were able to be as dynamic, you are putting yourself down and it can only lead to self-doubt.

We weren't all cut out to be dynamic experts. Gardeners, sales assistants, authors, mechanics, doctors, or any other profession or way of life, all bring a different quality to this world.

By knowing your limitations, and accepting what you can do, and what you can't, you will find peace. If you try to push yourself to be better, then you are sending the message to yourself that you're not good enough; you will be setting yourself up for failure. That's not to say you shouldn't be following a dream or working towards a desirable outcome. Just be happy where you are today, and enjoy the journey. The destination might be a let-down; all may not be as it seems, so why put all your eggs in that one basket.

By accepting your limitations, you will gain control of your life and the chasing will stop. I made myself miserable after writing my first couple of novels. I realised I had to learn how to market and I didn't have a clue. I struggled to try to take everything I learned on board. Why could everyone else manage and I couldn't? How did they all know so much about search engines and algorithms? Then I stopped trying so hard to be like everyone else and took it in my stride. Stress over. I do what I can, and guess what, nowadays I even manage to help answer other people's questions.

I took back control instead of worrying about what was expected of me, or should I say, what I expected of me. No one else was saying I couldn't do it, only that uninvited voice making me miserable. I made a choice. My dream is still in place and I'm sure that one day I'll look back and laugh. Now, I know my limitations, and I do what I feel comfortable with.

I have to admit that once I let go of the chase to get it right, to make something of myself, stopped trying to satisfy unrealistic expectations, I sailed.

I don't dwell on what I don't know, or can't do. I learn what I want to and take it at my own pace. My inner voice hasn't nagged me about my failings because there aren't any. I´m moving on at my own pace and enjoying every minute of it.

Exercise 2: Do you sometimes expect too much of yourself? Do you let other people's successes influence what you are doing? Take some time to consider if deep down you believe you are a failure or a success.

If you've answered yes to the questions, turn things around and accept your limitations. Maybe set smaller, working towards, manageable goals.

If you believe you are successful, great! If not, work on that. Ask why and find a way to change it. Love who you are, and start with you.

Chapter 3 - Courage

"Life is too short to not have fun…"

-Coolio

At the end of their lives, a lot of people wish they'd had the courage to go against what was expected of them and had lived life for themselves. Bronnie Ware wrote an article after offering palliative care to people at the end of their lives. Take a look at it here (that link is also at the end of the book). She found that people actually grew when they faced mortality. I'd suggest that by then they had nothing to lose. What a shame to wait so long.

The recurring regrets were:

- Not living a life true to themselves
- Working too hard
- Not expressing feelings
- Not staying in touch with friends
- Not allowing themselves to be happy

Having the courage to stand up for what we believe is not always easy.

Dictionary.com defines courage as:

(1) "the quality of mind or spirit that enables a person to face difficulty..."

(2) "have the courage of one's convictions to act in accordance with one's beliefs especially in spite of criticism."

The question is, do you want to live your own life or do you want to live in the shadow of what other's dictate. *I'm not brave*, I hear you say. *I just want a peaceful, quiet life.* Don't we all? The thing is, we are here on earth for a relatively short space of time and who wants to get to the end of their life or good health and suddenly realise it's too late to accomplish dreams?

Would you choose to be one of Bronnie Ware's patients, wishing things had been different? Of course not! Everything you do in life is a learning curve and there is no room for regret. What you choose to do at any given time, is a choice you made that seemed right at the time. Believe in what you did and why.

However, let's turn this around. I've talked a lot about choosing and making choices. What about the choices you didn't make? The chances you didn't take. Why wait until your health has deteriorated or your days are numbered and then regret the things you didn't do.

I'm not suggesting you trample over loved ones and friends to accomplish a dream, but your life is just that, yours. You owe it to yourself to undertake and enjoy a few ideas before it's too late. As Bronnie advocates, most people delay their dreams and make excuses, and then the time has gone.

As my regular readers already know, I love lists. Without fear of retribution, I dare you to imagine talking to a stranger, looking back on your life and the things you wish you'd done. Write them down. Do you have the courage?

The list shouldn't only be physical. It should include feelings, friendships, ambitions, and happiness.

Now, do you have the courage of your convictions to put a few of those ideas, dreams or regrets into practice? Not all of them, remember, know your limitations, but what steps could you take towards one of your ideas?

There are wonderful examples of people who have lived life to the full. One is Mohr Keet, who at 96, bungee jumped 708 feet from South Africa's Western Cape heralding him as the oldest bungee jumper. At the time, he also enjoyed white water rafting and parachuting!

Maybe your dreams aren't that energetic, but you should understand that it's never too late to do the things you want to do.

People around you might not always support you, but they have their own life and you have yours. Sometimes people have ulterior motives for wanting to stop you from doing something. They can blame the risks, your health, (their health when they worry over you) financial concerns, or and this is true, jealousy or love. Some people haven't got the drive to do what they want to do and they have a lot to say about people who follow their heart. If they can't find the strength to stand apart from the crowd, they might feel threatened by your intentions. These people have stopped dreaming and only do what's expected of them. Stand firm and believe in yourself. Show your inner courage and strength and do whatever it is that you want to do.

Laziness is another reason people don't follow their passions. It's too much effort to change anything. You don't have to jump in at the deep end, but a little splash around in the shallows will get you off to a great start.

Exercise 3: Write a list and start working towards your dreams while you have time. Who knows what tomorrow will bring.

Chapter 4 – Regrets

"It's better to look ahead and prepare, than to look back and regret."

-Jackie Joyner-Kersee

Our past makes us what we are, and determines how we feel about ourselves. Regrets set us up for a downfall. They taunt and nag, always there, never leaving us. They spoil the future and zap inner confidence if you allow them to. No one knows how things from the past felt for you, the torment they created, and the continuing emotions that turn into regrets.

We all have a storage tank, and that tank will just keep on getting deeper if you let it. I have heard of the mind being described as an iceberg with only a small piece, about 10%, above the surface. That means that 90% must be below the surface of the sea. If that hidden ice is compared to our minds, that's a lot of stuff going on below the surface. Scary!

So, if that 90% is our storage tank, a tank programmed to hold on to what you tell it to, then you can see where the problems stem from. But the key is, that a storage tank can't hold what you don't put in it. You are the only one who can decide what goes in your tank and what doesn't.

"Accept everything about yourself. I mean everything. You are you and that is the beginning and the end – no apologies, no regrets."

-Henry Kissinger

Our memories have such a lot to answer for. You might ask yourself why you keep thinking over and over again about a certain situation. You aren't thinking, you are remembering and most people tend to recall the less pleasant memories instead of the good ones. Your mind, yes, that inner voice again, replaying the hurt, the comment and the aftermath of how you felt.

So how do you begin to let go? By turning it around. If you read book one, Choose to Change: It's your life, then you'll be familiar with finding the positive; basically, turning negative thoughts into positive ones.

What did you learn from the things that you now deem as regrets? There must be one positive thing. Maybe you regret being weak in a certain situation. You learned that you should or could have been stronger. For whatever reason, you chose not to be stronger. If you regret not speaking your mind, you learned that you could have said what you felt you should have said, but something held you back. You chose not to speak up. You made a choice. Do you get the idea?

It doesn't matter how many regrets you have, you will have learned something from each one. Maybe you learned something enormous and life-changing, or maybe it was so small that you think it's insignificant.

The important thing here is that you don't have to have regrets. You have a learning curve, and that learning curve is positive. What's the saying about learning something new every day? The practice of learning is what deepens our character and makes us more confident.

"I wouldn't change anything. I think it's important to let things happen, and stay 'happened'. I think that's all part of the learning curve, part of fate."

-Mike Peters

Learn that you have a choice and stand by your decisions. You made them for good reason at the time.

When I look back on my life and think about some of the significant events, I realise that they set me up for what was to come. My mind works in a certain way due to past experiences. I first knew I had to start with me when my husband left me, and our daughter, who was only ten days old. It was devastating, but after the initial shock, I learned that I could manage. I was stronger than I thought, and that alone, gave me the strength to believe in myself and taught me how to be independent. I bounced back once I realised I was enough. A little antidote; he was a terrible husband and father, but always a friend. Yes, he let us down, but I couldn't change him and wouldn't have tried to. I was happy, and because I could let go, no gremlins were eating away at me. For those of you who are interested, when my daughter hit her teens, she spent as much time with her father as she did with me. He had horses and dog kennels!

No one can change history. What happened is in the past. All that's left is how you are going to deal with what happened on the inside. You are not defined by failure, the past, or what anyone says—it just points you in another direction.

So start refilling your storage tank with what you can do and what you have learned. It's time for a clear-out and a re-vamp.

Exercise 4: Write down a regret that taunts you. Now write the one thing you learned from that. Repeat with other regrets and set yourself free. Get that learning curve going and be someone who lives life to the full with no regrets. After all, life's too short for regrets.

"I'm not someone who dwells upon past events, taking the view that life is too short."

-Charles Kennedy

Chapter 5 – Confidence

"Low self-confidence isn't a life sentence. Self-confidence can be learned, practiced, and mastered—just like any other skill. Once you master it, everything in your life will change for the better."

-Barrie Davenport

Do you have confidence in yourself? How confident are you on the inside?

Do you worry about how other people see you? What they think about you? For most people, wanting to be liked comes with the territory. Have you ever considered why that is? If you love yourself and you're happy with who you are, you don't need other people to like you. They will though because when you love yourself, the rest will follow naturally. People will like your confidence and you will give off positive vibes that will draw people to you.

Confidence is not thinking, *people like me*; confidence is thinking, *it's fine if they don't like me.*

However, the truth is, that no one fits in with everyone; great people never do! Think about a recent film you've seen or a book you've read. Did you like all the characters equally or were you drawn to some more than others? It doesn't mean there was anything wrong with the ones you weren't drawn to unless they were perhaps a villain, a masked murderer or some other character trait that we are supposed to dislike.

The great thing is that we don't all have to be the same. You are the only you, so be proud of that. You don't need anyone else to make you whole. You were whole when you were born and you continue to be whole; you are complete!

My inner confidence has led me into deep waters on several occasions. I have never done what is expected of me and I've always had the confidence to stand by my convictions. As a result, people often refer to me as awkward because I don't follow the rules. I speak my mind and take risks—no one knows what's coming next; not even me! And do I care? No, not one little iota. It's me and if people can't accept me for who I am, there is nothing I can, or would want to do about that.

I don't think I am better than anyone else, but I accept myself, faults and all.

When you have confidence in yourself you will be stronger and your strength will continue to grow. To love yourself, you have to have an inner confidence. The good thing is that self-confidence can be learned, but like everything else in life, to be good at it, we have to practice, there is no quick fix.

Make a list of some things in your life that you have achieved. Up to ten would be good. Did someone thank you and say what a difference you made? Perhaps you rescued an animal. Did you pass an exam? Are you in charge of anything at work? Think about bringing up your children, if you have any. Was it a success for you? How about your listening skills? Your garden? Your friendships? Maybe your achievements go way beyond my suggestions. Don't hold back. List your achievements; anything that makes you a bit proud.

If you're struggling to make a list, think of some small thing you could do that might help someone else. It could be as simple as a message or phone call to see how someone is.

Keep looking at this list and remembering what you've done.

Consider what is important to you and what you want from life. Where do you want to be in ten years, five, or in a year's time? What about next month, in six months? Next week! Now I've got you thinking. Having goals and a plan will up your confidence. You will have a purpose and a vision for the future. Believe that you will achieve your goals.

Keep changing negative thoughts into positive ones. There is a chapter on this in book 1. Each time you have a negative thought and put yourself down, turn it into something positive. Negative - "I can't do this, I'm useless." Positive – "I bet I can do this if I try and put my mind to it. I just need to put in some effort."

Promise yourself that you will stay committed to your journey. That voice in your head is going to put you down. "You won't be able to, you can't, you're not capable, and so on." Write down what the voice is telling you and then calmly and rationally dispute the claims. If there is a reason you can't turn it around, make another small goal to counteract the problem. For example, if your plan is to go on holiday abroad next year, and your inner voice is telling you "it's impossible, you'll never afford it", you need a smaller plan in place with ideas to get the money saved. Just an example, but do you understand where I'm coming from?

Inner confidence is about getting the balance right. If you lack confidence you might avoid change, and take no risks. You might even not try to succeed. If you have too much confidence, you might take too many risks and be so optimistic that you don't try to succeed because you think it's a given.

This brings us back to knowing your limitations. With practice, you will stretch yourself and take risks within your abilities, and that is down to your confidence.

Exercise 5: Keep adding to your list of achievements and do keep looking at them. Be proud of who you are. Love yourself – be someone who makes you happy.

"There's only one person you're guaranteed to spend the rest of your life with… yourself."

-Bill Murray

Chapter 6 - Do you want anything enough?

"If you really want to do something, you'll find a way. If you don't, you'll find an excuse."

-Jim Rohn

In the last chapter, we touched on what you want and where you want to be in five years from now. You're reading this book, so it would be fair to assume you want something to change in your life. It could be any area of your life: health, relationship, career, social, financial, spiritual, personal development, or family; it could be any number of areas you would like to change.

The question is, how much do you want the change and how much effort are you prepared to put in to reach where you want to be?

If you're not committed to making changes, then you don't need to read any more of this book as it won't be able to help you.

If you're still reading – great!

The first thing is the plan. Maybe you wrote one when you read the last chapter. Now is the time to break it down into manageable steps. Let's take a health example. In one years' time, I want to be fit and partaking in lots of sports. I can't start by doing ten different sports; my body would be exhausted. So, I would plan to run half a mile every day, do some warming up exercises, and I might alter my diet. These would be my starting goals.

On day one, I struggle. Yes, I really would! So, I change my plan to run half a mile. Instead, I go for a half-mile healthy walk. Then I'd plan to up the walk to a short run and gradually increase what I do. Do you get the idea?

Having a SMART goal (specific, measurable, achievable, relevant, timely) allows you to keep track of where you are and how you are progressing.

Now sit down with a pad, or a journal and pen, and start to construct your personal goal or goals. I'd like you to do this before you carry on reading. If you skip this, you might forget to come back and do it.

"Let us make our future now, and let us make our dreams tomorrow's reality."

-Malala Yousafzai

The reality is that once you start, you are on the way, and wouldn't it be great to wake up tomorrow morning and know you've taken the first step.

So, now you have a goal, a plan to move you forward.

Time for reality to kick in! You won't get to your goal or your dream by having another cup of coffee. I promise you won't! It takes dedication and a lot of people in this world don't dedicate themselves and then wonder why they don't get what they want. You have to live it! You have to focus!

What is the one thing you can do today to get you closer to your goal? Remember why you want this, and go for it. Only you can do this. Follow your dream and start working towards it. Enjoy the journey as you'll learn a lot on the way and you might even surprise yourself.

Exercise 6: Every day focus on the one thing that will take you forward.

"Follow your passion, be prepared to work hard and sacrifice, and, above all, don't let anyone limit your dreams."

-Donovan Bailey

How are you doing?

Let's have a recap. By now, you should have taken some steps towards putting your inner voice in its rightful place with a gag in place.

You have considered your abilities and limitations and are no longer stressing over what you can't do and have a focus on what you can do. You've given up the chase and are instead, enjoying the journey.

You found courage, from somewhere deep down inside, and you are not going to let life pass you by without at least putting some of your dreams or wants into action.

You look at what used to be regrets as a learning curve. You've accepted your regrets are history, you learned from them and let them go. Life is too short.

You're looking at that list of things you're proud of and adding to it now and again. You're learning to love yourself for who you are.

You've decided on a goal. You have a plan in place and every day you do one thing to take you forward.

If you're not doing or haven't done some or any of these then I suggest re-reading and setting yourself on the road to loving yourself. You will feel better and reap untold rewards both environmentally and personally.

We're now heading into Part 2. Keep on rocking. Mmm! That brings back a memory of a Praying Mantis I saw, wanting lunch. He rocked backwards and forwards in a slow methodical rhythm. One tiny movement each time. The only reason I knew he was closing in on his prey (a fly) was because of the pattern on the tile. Such patience and perseverance. The one thing! And wham! He got it! One small step at a time.

Did you know that changing things can take up to 30 days to get used to? Make new habits that will last you a lifetime and you'll never look back. Keep going and make your dreams come true – tiny tweaks will get you there.

"We can do anything we want if we stick to it long enough."

-Helen Keller

Part 2 -

Chapter 7 - Happiness is inside you

"The only thing that will make you happy is being happy with who you are.

-Goldie Hawn

It really is. Happiness can't be bought or found. No one can make you happy. Other people can do nice things, but happiness is within and you have to choose to be happy.

Happiness can't come to you, only from you, so you need to make a conscious effort to unleash it. It sounds weird, but it's true. You have a choice and you can choose whether to be happy or not. It might take practice to change the way you think, but nothing is stopping you from doing that except you and your thoughts.

How do you draw out something that's been hidden away for a while? Do you even know where to look for it?

Start at the beginning. With you. That is what this book is all about. Now is a tough time for honesty. Ask yourself the question: What do I like about me? What do I dislike about myself? You can answer truthfully, only you will know the answer.

Take a few deep breaths to get you over the shock of those revelations. There must have been revelations or you'd be happy in the place you are already in, and you wouldn't be reading this book.

Look again at the things you don't like about yourself. It's all about loving yourself, and it's difficult to love someone if you don't like them. Not impossible, but just harder. Let's be honest, if there's something you don't like, it's going to cause friction and that inner voice is going to keep chipping away.

You'll unleash some happiness if you do something, anything, to change what you don't like. Nothing too drastic just tweaks to set you free from inner turmoil.

Does everything you do have a purpose? It doesn't matter if the purpose is small, as long as there is a purpose. Doing things with no purpose gives no satisfaction and therefore no joy. The purpose could be entertainment, financial, helpful, charitable, and the list goes on, as long as you have a purpose. Stop doing anything that has no purpose.

"When you dance, your purpose is not to get to a certain place on the floor. It's to enjoy each step along the way."
-Wayne Dyer

Having purpose releases the happiness within. Remember the purpose, the why, why you do what you do. If you don't like the answer, it might be time for another change.

A study, looking for the happiest people in the world and why they were happy, found that underprivileged people living in Siberia were amongst the happiest. They lived in shacks, with the main breadwinner hunting and gathering daily to put food on the table.

They were happy with each other, and with their lives. They were grateful for what they had. They had a purpose in everything they did. I've put a link to the YouTube documentary at the end of the book.

I also found this to be true when I lived in Mauritius. Yes, that's right, Mauritius. Away from the tourist industry at the Northern end of the island is an underdeveloped Southern area with some of the happiest people I have ever met. They fished to put food on the table, they helped each other, and most importantly, they were happy with what they had. They had a purpose in their lives. More about that in another book I'm writing, just in its primary stages at the moment.

"Happiness is not something you postpone for the future; it is something you design for the present."

-Jim Rohn

So now is the time to find your inner happiness. Never doubt yourself. Your happiness is waiting for you to release it. Always remember happiness is a choice, not a result.

"When unhappy, one doubts everything; when happy, one doubts nothing."

-Joseph Roux

Exercise 7: Search your inner-self. What is holding back your happiness? Write it down. Then write what you need to do to turn that around.

Chapter 8 - Are you fulfilled?

"Plant the seed of desire in your mind and it forms a nucleus with power to attract to itself everything needed for its fulfillment.

-Robert Collier

What does that mean? Do you feel there is more out there for you, but you just haven't found what it is yet? Where do you start looking for anything when you don't know what you're looking for? It all gets a bit confusing and doesn't help.

Being fulfilled is about finding what makes you tick, what makes you come alive, what you love doing. Holidays and weekends I hear you say, but I'm talking about in your life. Every day, what is your thing?

What has you so engrossed that you don't realise what the time is? Is there something that makes you miss meal times and only your stomach rumbling reminds you to eat?

Television doesn't count as an answer; turn it off! When do you lose yourself?

If you don't have anything that makes you feel alive, then that is what's missing. Cast your mind back to your childhood. What did you love to do? Did you have a hobby? Did adults say you wasted too much time doing something you loved?

For me, I used to run a pretend library. I had little tickets in front of every one of my books and there were lots of them. I also had a torch hidden away so I could read at night when I was supposed to be sleeping. I used to have pen-friends from Peru, Italy, Spain and Germany. My childhood was spent on anything related to books and writing. I also loved dogs as a child and have rarely been without a four-legged friend all my life. I have ten at the moment. I also lived by the sea, which was and still is, a great love of mine.

So I'm still doing what I loved as a child. Those passions just grew stronger, they never left me. I feel fulfilled in my life because I'm surrounded by things that I love and love to do.

When I had children, I didn't stop my passions. My children grew up on the coast, we always had dogs, although I have to admit my reading time did take a blow, but the important thing is that I never let my passions slip away; even though my life changed dramatically, I never grew out of my passions, they never left me.

Why would anyone believe that they grow out of their passions? Yes, you move on and sometimes you stop doing something because you don't want to continue, but that is completely different to giving something up for someone else or just simply not bothering to do what fulfils you.

"Musicians must make music, an artist must paint, a poet must write if he is to be ultimately at peace with himself. What a man can be, he must be."

-**Abraham Maslow**

Maslow studied happiness and was one of the first psychologists to do this. For him, self-actualisation was to live life to the full and realise your abilities. He advocated that anxiety and stress can be side effects when there is a lack of stimulation of the mind.

Your mind needs exercise and satisfaction just like your muscles need to build up to carry you. If your mind isn't fulfilled – how can you be happy within yourself?

To continue with Maslow's findings, he believed that you always have two choices. Step forward or stay safe. If you take even small steps forward you will be self-actualising, but if you continue to stay safe, you can't make progress that will fulfil you.

So, maybe you already know what fulfils you. If not, search back until you find times when you have been engrossed. If you can't think of anything you loved but stopped doing, how about trying a few new things?

If money wasn't an issue, what would you be doing? How could you work towards doing something you love?

Will you take a step forward or are you going to stay in the safe zone and wish you felt more fulfilled?

Exercise 8: Write down the things you have enjoyed. Even if you can't go back to swinging from the monkey bars at the park, there must be something you can do to relive those memories.

"By striving to do the impossible, man has always achieved what is possible. Those who have continuously done no more than they believe possible have never taken a single step forward."

-Mikhail Bakunin

Chapter 9 - What are you going to do?

"If you're searching for that one person that will change your life, take a look in the mirror."

-Unknown

The title of this chapter is an easy question to ask, but is there an easy answer? Yes. Simply start believing in yourself. Start loving yourself and life will take on more meaning. You won't be searching for answers; you won't need to because the answers are all in you already, you just have to release them.

Have faith in yourself, I can't stress this enough. Loving yourself will give you strength. Why put your happiness in someone else's pocket when it's right there in your pocket and always has been? Don't wait for someone to give you flowers; plant your own seeds.

Life changes are about integrating habits into your life so that within time the habits become natural. But you have to start somewhere.

Having other people tell you that you're loved and that they're proud of you is great and it makes you feel good. Why wait for those rare comments to make your day? Other people don't often spend their time throwing random compliments your way, they just don't. It doesn't mean they don't love you or aren't proud, it just means that now and again a compliment comes your way and for a while it makes you feel good, but it doesn't happen often enough to have a lasting effect.

So how about doing it for yourself? It doesn't matter where you are or what you're doing, tell yourself, *I'm proud of you, you managed that, I love you, well done...* You don't have to shout it from the rooftops, it can be a silent message to self, but a consistent one. A message to remind yourself that you're doing well and you're loved.

You have created you. The way you have taken past experiences and translated them, what you have learned from them and taken on board, it's all added up to make you who you are. When people have said something or you've dealt with a situation, you have put your own meaning on that experience. You have believed that someone meant something by what they said and that thought has stayed with you. It's true. We all interpret and take what we want from every experience.

So, start with you! If you told yourself that you loved you, what are you going to take from that? Okay, the first few times it'll feel strange. It's not something you'd want to share with everyone, but given time and consistency, you are going to believe what you hear and things will start to get better. This book is all about loving yourself, and if you never have, it's going to take a while to get used to it and then Ker-boom, you're on a new path and there'll be no stopping you.

You don't have to believe me, I already know, so it doesn't make any difference to me if you believe it or not, but you have to start believing in yourself. Telling yourself that you love yourself is the first step in the plan.

Start right now and then carry on. If those doubts creep in, knock them back with 'I love you'. Three little words that can impact your life and make such a difference.

"Love yourself first and everything else falls into place. You really have to love yourself to get anything done in this world."

-Lucille Ball

Tell yourself all the time and keep doing it. You won't have a choice about whether you believe it or not, you just will, and then your happiness will flood out. This is the one thing to start the biggest change and the one thing that is going to make your life so different.

Exercise 9: Pay yourself compliments and say those three little words 'I love you'. Repeat! Repeat! Repeat!

Chapter 10 - Are you in the system?

"The pessimist complains about the wind. The optimist expects it to change. The realist adjusts the sail."

-William A Ward

I often describe people as *in the system*. It refers to those people who conform to what's expected of them. Usually, they like to moan and put the world to rights, although they're not prepared to do anything much about it themselves. Dare I say, these people are often grumps with no vision of a mind-blowing future ahead, in fact, they are often pessimists who are never happy?

People who are *in the system* can't see a bright future for themselves, or anyone else. I have to say, as soon as I come into contact with anyone *in the system* I make a hasty retreat; I find them toxic.

If you are in the system – you need to leave right now!

No one makes the choice, at least not consciously, to join the system. That's to say, I hope no one would make that decision. People just fall into the trap and before they know it – bop! There they are, moaning and groaning, and bringing themselves down, along with anyone else who will listen.

I know a man, a neighbour, who I don't bump into very often, who can find negativity and something to moan about on any subject. I do not jest! The weather: too hot, cold, windy, no air, cloudy, not a cloud, you get the idea. He doesn't know he does it. I asked him about it once and he almost smiled and said he only complained when there was something to complain about. He wasn't offended, but sat deep in thought for a while and then actually laughed. *'You know, you're right. It's not often I have anything good to say. I'm going to make an effort.'* I thanked him and since then I've seen a new side to him. His greeting is always cheery and he looks, dare I say it, happier. I honestly don't know if he only makes an effort when he sees *me* or if he's changed his whole outlook. He needs to read my book!

I've added this chapter now because if you have followed any of the advice in this book, even if you started off in the system, by now you should have moved on.

Look at the people around you. Are they in the system? If so, you are not doing yourself any favours by spending too long in their company.

Numerous studies have found that happy people are healthier, especially their immune system, they excel at work, and they are popular, meaning they have more friends.

Happy people are not constrained by the rules society places on them. They have a life and they live it, often contributing to the happiness of others. Be one of life's givers, spread happiness and turn around other people's moans and groans. You don't have to agree with them, and it will have a knock-on effect.

Exercise 10: Don't complain about anything for a day. If that's too long, start with I hour and build up to a day. You will be amazed at the difference it makes.

"I'm not going to hold my breath because life goes on. Life is too short to sit around moaning about what could have been or what was."

-Tina Weymouth

Chapter 11 – Meditation

"The thing about meditation is: You become more and more you."

-David Lynch

I wanted to add a short chapter about meditation. There are hundreds of books that focus on meditation, so I'm not going to go into it in a big way, and I've never read a meditation book. But meditation did make a huge difference in my life and I'd like to share that experience with you.

Years ago, I was in a bad place and was willing to try anything to set myself free from the inner torment. I'm sure that awful time in my life will be written in a book one day, but not yet.

I read, played tennis, took my dogs for long walks and really tried to pull myself up. Then I read an article about Transcendental Meditation (TM) and I was hooked. The class was run by Colin Beckley, founder of the Meditation Trust, and his classes were not too far from where I lived.

I went along; in those days he held the classes in the front room at his home. I learned how to meditate, following the heart of the yoga system the world's most ancient system of personal development and natural healthcare.

The following is an extract from The Meditation Trust website.

'By dissolving the stress which distorts our personality, TM reduces our negative habits of thought, speech or action, leaving room for the real, wonderful you to shine through! Whilst being calmer inside, you will tend to find yourself more self-assertive, self-confident and alert, many people have. No change of personality – just more in balance.

Most of us enjoy some challenge in our lives which increases motivation and helps us achieve great things. But we all have a point (which varies from person to person) where that challenge can become pressure, and counter-productive. When you're tired, feeling stressed and under pressure, you're more likely to make mistakes.

Creativity comes from being clear-minded, calm and rested. The *yogis* of India have for thousands of years described the silence of <u>meditation</u> as a state of 'restful alertness', wide awake but still. When this quality is brought to the surface level of the mind after meditation, it replaces the nervous tension that so many had been relying on previously for stimulation. This has been an absolute revelation for thousands of meditators, who have found themselves more creative, clear headed, successful and stress-free as a result.

After I'd completed the course, I couldn't see much change or so I thought. Then one day, standing at the bedroom mirror, I saw the old me. The person who didn't have those stress lines and that fraught look on her face. I knew I was in a good place again. I'd set myself free, well, with Colin's help, and I realised that things in my life were settled once again. I was relaxed and accepting of people and situations around me.

I was so cross I'd missed the moment, not really cross, more peeved, but I did have to wonder how such a huge transformation had taken place without me realising.

I don't profess to know any more than I was taught, but those teachings have stayed with me and to this day I still meditate and more importantly, with everything life throws at me, I'm still happy. Don't misunderstand, I don't have a perfect life, and I don't know anyone who does. What I do have, is the ability to assess situations with a calm outlook and take things in my stride.

As I said earlier, there are lots of books on meditation and if you're in the UK, I seriously recommend you get yourself booked onto one of Colin's courses. I don't know the difference between, for example, Mindfulness and TM, but I do know TM worked for me and I've never looked back. If you aren't in the UK, I believe there are TM classes and centres all over the world, so it'd be worth looking one up or take a trip of a lifetime to the UK, you only have one life. Go for it!

Exercise 11: Meditate. Sit somewhere quiet and comfortable. Close your eyes and your mind to everything around you. Repeat a sound in your mind. (Not a word, a sound. For example: ee-em, be-ra. I made those up. Make up a sound you like that doesn't make you link to anything). Repeat the sound in your head. If you mind wanders, and it will, come back to the sound. Focus on nothing but the sound. (Don't say anything out aloud). Twenty minutes is a good time to spend freeing your mind. This is the meditation I use.

Chapter 12 - Obstacles or Opportunities

"Whenever you want to achieve something, keep your eyes open, concentrate and make sure you know exactly what it is you want. No one can hit their target with their eyes closed."

-Paulo Coelho

So, let's consider for a moment, that if everything is already in us, how do we find it? How do we unleash it, because if it was easy, surely we'd have found a way?

I know I keep saying this, but it's the meaning you give to situations, it's your reaction that determines the outcome. You have a choice and only you can change anything in your life.

Are you focusing on opportunities or obstacles? In other words, what you want or what you don't want? Are you looking at ways to move forward or is your focus on what is holding you back? The way you look at situations will influence what happens around you.

Now we're back to loving who you are and treating yourself with the respect and compassion you deserve. You need to give yourself the chance to focus on where you want to be, not what is stopping you from getting there. Love is a strong force and will give you the strength to make changes and stick to them.

Emotions are a part of us all, but don't let them limit where you want to be or what you want to do. Nothing is cast in stone so everything is changeable; if you want it to, change it will.

If you change your outlook, new things will begin to happen. So what is one small thing you can do to get you closer to where you want to be?

As we discussed, in an earlier chapter, focusing on the one thing you care about, the one most important thing that will take you away from past inhibitions and forward with a new meaning that will positively impact your life.

Stop focusing on conflict and let yourself live in peace because you are the only one who can do that and nothing is going to improve if you don't let it, if you don't give it a chance.

"Don't dwell on what went wrong. Instead, focus on what to do next. Spend your energies on moving forward toward finding the answer."

-Denis Waitley

Consider for a moment that you are walking along in open-toe shoes and a tiny bit of grit somehow works its way under your foot. It niggles, it's uncomfortable and in the end, you have to stop to get rid of it spoiling your day, and maybe giving you a sore foot. When you take off your shoe, there is the tiniest bit of grit. How could something so small make you that uncomfortable and have such an impact that it managed to slow you down until, in the end, it stopped you altogether?

That's similar to the way little things impact our lives. In our minds, little tiny bits and pieces spoil our lives. But just like getting rid of the grit in your shoe, you can get rid of the particles in your mind that infringe on your life.

So, decide to stop putting obstacles in your way and instead fill the space with opportunity. What is the one thing that will allow you to move on, to feel good about yourself, to love yourself?

What is going to be your focus? Without a focus, you'll be stumbling around not sure which direction to head in. Do it today. Search out your focus and stick to it in all you do.

"I don't focus on what I'm up against, I focus on my goals and I try to ignore the rest."

-Venus Williams

Exercise 12: Make that decision – no more obstacles, only opportunities, and start today. Focus.

Chapter 13 – Shame

"A moment of self-compassion can change your entire day. A string of such moments can change the course of your life."

-**Christopher K. Germer**

Why do we feel shame? Shame is the difference between falling apart or feeling good. It's about staying indoors on a wet day, or putting on your wellies and getting out there.

Shame and guilt – we all do it so well, we're all so good at it.

Do you know there are no shame police, or guilt or failure police for that matter? No one has the authority to judge you, only you. Unless you're a criminal, of course.

So get real – you are enough. You can do this. You don't need perfection, that's only an excuse to protect yourself.

Guilt, shame and failure only exist in your mind. We return to that inner voice that keeps popping up. Why are others better than me? They are not. They are not! That isn't a typo, I wanted to say it twice so you didn't miss it.

Remember the chapter about regrets that turn into learning curves, well, I'm singing from that box again. Shame, guilt, losses, failure, regrets, I could go on, they all come under the same umbrella and they are not real, they are directional, in that they take you or lead you in another direction. Love yourself and be at ease.

The thing that caused you to feel shame or guilt, is who you think you should be, not who you are. The real you, did, said, acted, whatever, in the way you did for a reason and that reason is because that's the real you.

Love yourself for that. No one else knows what it's like to be you so don't feel guilty.

Change your priorities and work out the why. Why do you feel shame and guilt?

Those answers will be there. You need to find them and confront them.

Give yourself some constructive criticism about the why, and then move on. Free yourself and start to live. Get out there and dance like there is only you watching because, at the end of the day, it is only you who is important. The world, your world, begins and ends with you; so get out there and be proud.

Exercise 13: Every time you feel guilt creeping in, ask yourself why. You're entitled to speak your mind, have a bad day, or whatever. Give yourself a break. Tiny tweaks.

"An exciting and inspiring future awaits you beyond the noise in your mind, beyond the guilt, doubt, fear, shame, insecurity and heaviness of the past you carry around."

-Debbie Ford

Chapter 14 - Questions to ask yourself

I've asked a lot of questions and I hope you've answered some, if not all, of them. I thought it might be helpful to list a few that you can answer on a sheet of paper. The only stipulation is that you answer truthfully in full sentences with examples where possible. Yes, and no answers are not going to help you and neither is not being honest. As you answer each question, add why or what.

Are you true to yourself?

Do you believe your inner voice when it's unkind?

Do you have a plan for your life? What is it?

Are you envious of others?

Do you think you are the only one who struggles?

Do you expect too much of yourself?

Do you have confidence in yourself?

Did you learn from your regrets?

What have been your successes and achievements?

What do you want?

What can you do today to get closer to your goal?

Do you know what is holding you back?

Are you doing things that make you tick? What?

If money wasn't an issue, what would you be doing?

Do you believe in yourself?

Are you a moaner?

Do you focus on opportunity?

Do you love yourself?

We ended on the big question. Now I'd like you to go back over your answers, and, without excuses, make a note next to things that need to change to bring you closer to being happy with yourself.

"One of the most important decisions you will ever make is choosing the kind of universe you exist in: is it helpful and supportive or hostile and unsupportive? Your answer to this question will make all the difference in terms of how you live your life and what kind of divine assistance you attract."

-Wayne Dyer

Do you live in a helpful and supportive world, or a hostile and unsupportive world? I'll let you into a secret… They are the same place and you get to choose how you live in your world. Make your world the place you want to be.

Exercise 14: What small step can you take towards changing the things you're not happy with? Start working through your list.

Note: Only work on one area at a time. Make a small change and when you feel happier, move onto the next area. Start with something easy, and give yourself a timely goal. Tiny tweaks – always.

Chapter 15 – Conclusion

I probably could go on forever, but I hope by now you at least know where I'm coming from and where you're heading for.

You need to accept yourself for who you are, not what you or anyone else, thinks you should be. That means not trying to be a better person, you are already good enough.

Start with you. Love who you are and accept yourself as a friend – remember, you are your own best friend so be nice to yourself. That voice in your head can be a good thing too. It's there, we've all got one, so you might as well make it worthwhile listening to it and make sure it's telling you things that you want to hear.

Do not ever fixate on perfection or you'll be disappointed. Nothing is perfect. Know your limitations and be proud.

Get that plan going and focus on the here and now. It's only this moment in your life that is important, the rest will fall into place if you focus on letting go of feeling bad and start focusing on feeling good.

How many passions have you taken up again? You might laugh at yourself if you tried all of them. There is no way I'm swinging by my knees on the monkey bars in Carlton Avenue park, nor will I be putting little cards in the front of all my books so I can run a library that no one ever borrows a book from. Oh, and did those pen friends understand a single word when I undertook direct translations? Probably not! But what I'm saying is, find and rekindle some of your passions from your childhood, even if you've moved on.

Try some meditation, relax your mind and grab opportunities when they come.

I sincerely hope this little book has gone some way to help you understand what you can do if you want things in your life to change. The main thing you can take away is that whatever you want is already in you, and you just have to focus on releasing it.

If you've got to the end of this short book, and feel nothing has or will ever change, I implore you to keep on down the road to recovery. Nothing happens without practice, and with practice, you will arrive at your destination, but make sure you enjoy the journey.

"True life is lived when tiny changes occur."

-Leo Tolstoy

***

If you have enjoyed Choose to Count: Start with you, then you'll love my next book in the series, Choose to Create: Make the day yours: A plan for getting your day off to a good start. Go and take a look on Amazon now.

Thank you for reading Choose to Count. If you have gained anything from this book and you think it might help someone else, please do leave a review.

Your Checklist

Here's the link to copy into your browser for your Start with you Checklist PDF: https://dl.bookfunnel.com/z8t0siehxs

If you have any trouble getting your checklist, please contact me at: jacquipennauthor@gmail.com

You will be added to my readers group and I'll let you know about new releases, offers, and other news. I'll never share your information and you can unsubscribe at any time. The checklist is yours to keep as a thank you for taking an interest in my books.

Exercise List

Exercise 1: Challenge your inner voice every time it puts you down, and stop believing what it tells you. Make this small step towards loving and accepting who you are.

Exercise 2: Do you sometimes expect too much of yourself? Do you let other people's successes influence what you are doing? Take some time to consider if deep down you believe you are a failure or a success.

If you've answered yes to the questions, turn things around and accept your limitations. Maybe set smaller, working towards, manageable goals.

If you believe you are successful, great! If not, work on that. Ask why and find a way to change it. Love who you are, and start with you.

Exercise 3: Write a list and start working towards your dreams while you have time. Who knows what tomorrow will bring.

Exercise 4: Write down a regret that taunts you. Now write the one thing you learned from that. Repeat with other regrets and set yourself free. Get that learning curve going and be someone who lives life to the full with no regrets. After all, life's too short for regrets.

Exercise 5: Keep adding to your list of achievements and do keep looking at them. Be proud of who you are. Love yourself – be someone who makes you happy.

Exercise 6: Every day focus on the one thing that will take you forward.

Exercise 7: Search your inner-self. What is holding back your happiness? Write it down. Then write what you need to do to turn that around.

Exercise 8: Write down the things you have enjoyed. Even if you can't go back to swinging from the monkey bars at the park, there must be something you can do to relive those memories.

Exercise 9: Pay yourself compliments and say those three little words 'I love you'. Repeat! Repeat! Repeat!

Exercise 10: Don't complain about anything for a day. If that's too long, start with I hour and build up to a day. You will be amazed at the difference it makes.

Exercise 11: Meditate. Sit somewhere quiet and comfortable. Close your eyes and your mind to everything around you. Repeat a sound in your mind. (Not a word, a sound, for example: ee-em, be-ra. I made those up. Make up a sound you like that doesn't make you link to anything). Repeat the sound in your head. If you mind wanders, and it will, come back to the sound. Focus on nothing but the sound. (Don't say anything out aloud). Twenty minutes is a good time to spend freeing your mind. This is the meditation I use.

Exercise 12: Make that decision – no more obstacles, only opportunities, and start today. Focus.

Exercise 13: Every time you feel guilt creeping in, ask yourself why. You're entitled to speak your mind, have a bad day, or whatever. Give yourself a break. Tiny tweaks.

Exercise 14: What small step can you take towards changing the things you're not happy with? Start working through your list.
Note: Only work on one area at a time. Make a small change and when you feel happier, move onto the next area. Start with something easy, and give yourself a timely goal. Tiny tweaks – always.

Links

Bronnie Ware Regrets of the dying

http://www.bronnieware.com/blog/regrets-of-the-dying

Happy people (natural living off the land)

https://www.youtube.com/watch?v=fbhPIK-oBvA

The Meditation Trust

https://www.meditationtrust.com/

Acknowledgements

My heartfelt thanks to Glinys Graham, Susette Butler, and Nola Cooper for their continuous help and support.

I thank Clare King for her enthusiasm, ideas, and prompts which add so much to my books. You're a star!

Colin Beckley, where would I be without you? When you introduced me to meditation, I never thought for a moment it would impact my life like it has. Thank you from me and all the people I am now able to help.

About Jacqui

Jacqui Penn spends her time between Kent, England, and the Andalusian hillsides in Spain. When she's not writing, she can be found walking her dogs and mulling over ideas for her next book.

Through life's many ups and downs she has always managed to be a survivor, and believes a positive approach will conquer most of life's challenges.

Other Books by Jacqui Penn

Choose to Change: It's your life (Book 1)

Choose to Create: Start your day (Book 3)

Choose to Commit: Make new habits stick (Book 4)

This Year I Shall… An easy and proven system for making good habits stick (A journal for Book 4)

Choose to Change Journal (For Book 1)

A Year of Uplifting Inspiration

https://www.jacquipenn.co.uk

www.facebook.com/jacquipennauthor

https://twitter.com/jacquipenn

www.pinterest.com/jacquipenn1

Printed in Great Britain
by Amazon